The Missions of California

Mission Santa Cruz

Kim Ostrow

The Rosen Publishing Group's
PowerKids Press™
New York

To the Waxbates—for listening and listening and listening...

Published in 2000 by The Rosen Publishing Group, Inc.
29 East 21st Street, New York, NY 10010

Photo Credits and Photo Illustrations: pp. 1, 5, 11, 29, 48, 49, 50, 51, by Cristina Taccone; pp. 4, 40 © Superstock; pp. 7, 46, 47 CORBIS/Bettmann; p. 8 Courtesy of National Park Service, Cabrillo National Monument; pp. 10, 17 The Granger Collection, New York; p. 12 © Photo Disc; pp. 13, 16, 18, 19, 21, 22, 30 by Michael K. Ward; p. 20 © Shirley Jordan; p. 23 © Gil Cohen; p. 25 CORBIS/Bettmann; pp. 27, 44 © Department of Special Collections, University of Southern California Libraries; pp. 28, 50 Courtesy of Mission Santa Cruz; p. 35 © Art Resource; p. 36 © Schalkwijk/Art Resource; p. 48 © Santa Barbara Mission Archive - Library; pp. 52, 57 by Christine Innamorato.

First Edition

Book Design: Danielle Primiceri

Layout: Michael de Guzman

Editorial Consultant Coordinator: Karen Fontanetta, M.A., Curator, Mission San Miguel Arcángel
Editorial Consultant: Ruben G. Mendoza, Ph.D.
Institute of Archaeology, California State University, Monterey Bay
Associate Professor, Institute Director
Historical Photo Consultants: Thomas L. Davis, M. Div., M.A.
Michael K. Ward, M.A.

Ostrow, Kim.
Mission Santa Cruz / by Kim Ostrow.
p. cm. — (The missions of California)
Includes index.
Summary: The history of this California mission from its founding in 1791, through its development and use in serving the Ohlone Indians, and its secularization and function today.
ISBN 0-8239-5499-4 (lib. binding)
1. Santa Cruz Mission—History Juvenile literature. 2. Spanish mission buildings—California—Santa Cruz Region—History Juvenile literature. 3. Franciscans—California—Santa Cruz Region—History Juvenile literature. 4. Ohlone Indians—Missions—California—Santa Cruz Region—History Juvenile literature. 5. California—History—To 1846 Juvenile literature. [1. Santa Cruz Mission—History. 2. Missions—California. 3. Ohlone Indians—Missions. 4. Indians of North America—Missions—California. 5. California—History—To 1846.] I. Title. II. Series.
F869.S48 O88 1999 99-24609
979.4'71—dc21 CIP

Manufactured in the United States of America

Contents

The Spanish in the Age of Exploration

Mission Santa Cruz

Today, the small, busy city of Santa Cruz is filled with schools, libraries, shops, homes, and parks. Santa Cruz also has something that might not be visible right away—a rich and exciting history. On Mission Hill, just a few blocks away from the downtown area, stands a small, one-story building. At first glance, there is not much to see. The walls are white. The roof is red. There is nothing fancy about its appearance. Within the walls of this building, though, lies the beginning of the city of Santa Cruz. Also there, lies a piece of the dramatic history of the state of California. It is the story of missionaries and soldiers, pirates and settlers. It is a tale of religion and power, cooperation and cruelty. This modest structure is the last remaining building of Mission Santa Cruz, and all this history now rests within its walls.

The Spanish Come to the Americas

In 1492, after Christopher Columbus brought back news of what he called the New World (North America, South America, and Central America), the Spanish

Columbus brought the first news of the Americas to Spain.

The city of Santa Cruz has grown and developed around the mission that was built there in the 1700s.

government was eager to explore the land further. The Spanish were hoping to find gold, great cities to conquer, or a faster trade route to Asia, where they could buy silks and spices to sell for high prices in Europe.

In 1519, a Spanish soldier and explorer named Hernán Cortés brought ships, guns, horses, and soldiers to the land that today is Mexico, and there, in 1521, he conquered the great Aztec Empire for Spain. Spain named this land New Spain and set up a government under an official called a viceroy, who would act in place of the king. The Spanish quickly established towns in New Spain, but they wanted to expand their empire even more. In 1542, Viceroy Mendoza of New Spain sent an explorer named Juan Rodríguez Cabrillo up the

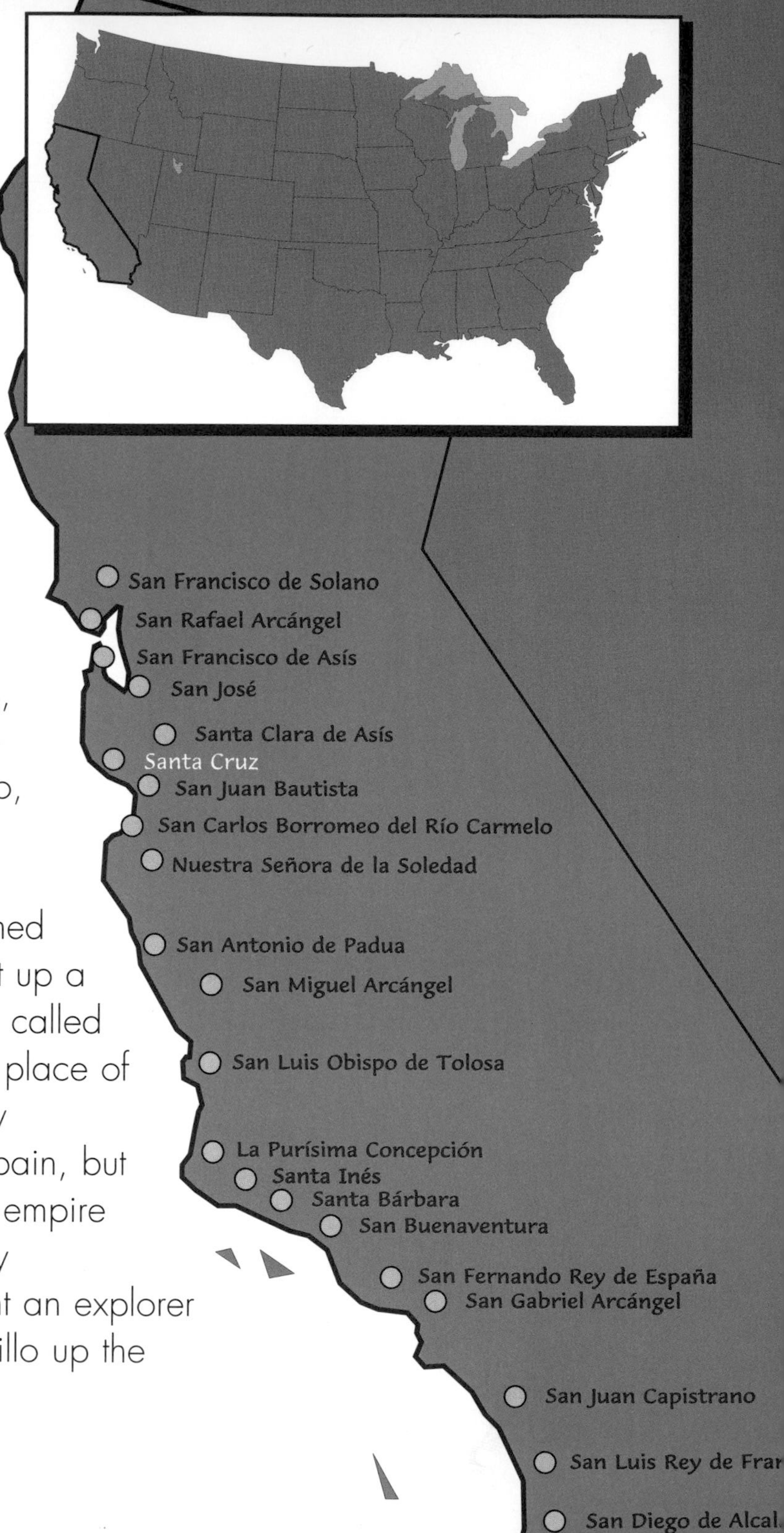

California coast in search of a river that cut through North America to Asia. He hoped that this would be the trade route that the Spanish had dreamed of and would bring them great riches. Cabrillo did not find the river (in fact, there is no such river), but instead, he found the harbor that today is San Diego Bay. Harbors were important because they allowed the ships to get close enough to shore so that men could get out and explore the land. When Cabrillo returned, he told of the harbor he had found and the land he had explored. Since he hadn't found riches, the land didn't sound valuable enough to the viceroy to send more ships there. The Spanish would not return to Alta California for 160 years.

Cortés conquered the Aztecs and claimed their land for Spain. Today, this land is Mexico.

The Mission System

When the viceroy of New Spain finally did decide to send more men to Alta California, it was because the Russians and British were beginning to make moves to settle there and claim the land. The Spanish wanted to make sure that Alta California would always belong to them. On January 9, 1769, the first of three ships carrying supplies set out for the harbor that Cabrillo had found in Alta California. Four months later, on May 15, a group of men began their journey on horseback over land to meet the ships.

Cabrillo was the first explorer to travel to Alta California for Spain.

When the Spanish conquered the Aztecs and established New Spain, they learned a lot about settling a land where people already lived. They felt that it was better to try to get along with the people who lived there than to fight with them. Because they were invading other people's land, getting along might prove to be difficult. The Spanish discovered that getting along was easier if they set up religious missions. A mission is a place where religious leaders teach others about their religion. By sending missionaries to teach the American Indians about Spanish religion and culture, they could get the Indians to begin to think and act more like them. This would prevent people in the Americas from wanting to fight against the Spanish, and Spain would have an easier time colonizing the land.

At this time in history, neither the Spanish who colonized California nor the other groups of Europeans who settled in the original 13 colonies valued diversity. Most Europeans believed that people of other races were not as smart or as developed as the Europeans themselves. They also believed that the Christian religion was the only right religion and that European cultures were the best cultures. These were the ideas that led to the great expansion of European empires and to the terrible destruction of other peoples and cultures.

The Spanish were Catholics, and the men they sent as missionaries when they colonized Alta California were a group of Catholics called Franciscan friars, or *frays* in Spanish. Although the Spanish government wanted to build missions to help claim more land for Spain, the Franciscan friars went to the missions because they wanted to help people. At this time, the Catholics thought that anyone who did not believe in Christianity would be punished after death. The friars became missionaries because they wanted to teach people to believe in Christianity so that they could go to heaven.

One of the men included in the May 15th journey over land to Alta California was a Franciscan friar named Junípero Serra. King Carlos III of Spain sent Serra to

Fray Serra was the first president of the Alta California missions.

this new land because he was a devoted priest who had dedicated his life to teaching people in New Spain about his religion. Serra had been very successful in New Spain, converting many Indians to Christianity. He was therefore chosen as president of the Alta California missions that would be built along the Pacific coast. Fray Serra's enthusiasm for his work was so great that he would eventually found nine missions before his death in 1784. After Fray Serra died, Fray Fermín Francisco de Lasuén became president of the Alta California missions. It was Fray Lasuén who would eventually found Mission Santa Cruz.

In all, 21 missions were built along the California coast between July 1769 and July 1823. The story of these missions is an important part of the history of California, as well as of the entire United States of America.

Fray Lasuén founded Mission Santa Cruz in 1791.

The Ohlone Indians

Before Fray Lasuén and his men arrived to found Mission Santa Cruz, this area was filled with hillsides and prairies, swampland, beaches, and tall oak and redwood forests. Living throughout the area were many different Indian tribes. Today, these tribes are known as the Ohlone. The name Ohlone was originally the name of just one tribe that lived on the coastline of California, near Pescadero. That tribe's name is now used to describe the California Indians who lived around the bay area of San Francisco.

Acorns

Like most California Indians, the Ohlone lived by hunting and gathering. All the food they needed could be found in the local forests, prairies, and bodies of water. The forests were filled with acorns, which were a staple of the Ohlone diet. In the fall, every member of the tribe helped gather acorns from the oak trees. Using large wooden sticks, the Ohlone men hit the oak branches to knock the acorns to the ground. The women and children stood nearby, ready to gather them in baskets. After the acorns had been collected, the women laid them out to dry in the sun.

Acorns were an important source of nutrition for many California Indians.

The Ohlone lived on the coast.

Ohlone women used acorns to make flour for bread.

Once the acorns were dry and ready for storage, they were placed in a storehouse, where they would be safe from hungry animals. The tribe could not eat the acorns immediately because acorns have some poison in them. In order to remove the poison and make the acorns safe to eat, the women prepared them in a special way. First, they ground the acorns between two stones, called a mortar and pestle. Then, they poured boiling water over the crushed acorns 10 times. This removed the poison, making the acorns ready to use for cooking. The Ohlone women boiled them to make a thick cereal or used the flour to make bread.

Hunting and Gathering

The Ohlone gathered other food, too. Women were responsible for finding and picking fruits and vegetables. They gathered strawberries, grapes, mushrooms, carrots, and onions.

The men of the tribe hunted ducks and other birds, rabbits, antelopes, and deer. They also caught seafood in the Pacific Ocean and in nearby rivers. The Ohlone respected the land around them. They only hunted or caught what they needed to survive. When a member of the tribe killed an animal for food, he said a prayer for the animal. The Ohlone believed that this prayer would allow the animal to be reborn someday.

Ohlone men fished with spears or nets.

Buildings and Shelter

The Ohlone built their homes out of willow branches. They started by placing long branches into the ground and tying the tops together to form a roof in the shape of a dome. They wove branches through the sides to create walls. A small hole was left in the roof to allow smoke from a small cooking fire to escape. These homes varied in size and could be anywhere from 6 to 20 feet wide. Sometimes more than one family shared a home. These houses were meant to last for only one season. The Ohlone were nomadic, which means they did not live in one place for a long time. In order to survive, they had to move to find the best food source for the time of year. Sometimes, the Ohlone reused the willow frames from their homes if they returned to the same spot the next year.

The temescal *was used before hunts and ceremonies.*

Every village had a sweathouse, called a *temescal*. This was a small building with a pit dug in the ground for a fire. Men and boys sat close to the fire to make themselves sweat. After sweating, they would cool down in the local river. This was done to keep clean. It was also said that this practice cured many illnesses. The Ohlone used the *temescal* before religious ceremonies and other special occasions.

Clothing and Body Decorations

The men and boys of the Ohlone tribe wore little or no clothing in the warmer months. Women and girls wore beautifully decorated aprons. Both men and women wore deer or rabbit skin cloaks when it turned cold. Ohlone men and women wore earrings and nose rings made of shells, and necklaces made of both shells and feathers. They wore their hair piled on top of their heads. Both men and women painted lines and dots on their faces.

▲ *Ohlone Indians often painted their bodies for decoration.*

▲
The Ohlone Indians traded things with people from nearby areas.

Trading and Baskets

Trading was a very important and respected job in the Ohlone tribe. Since there were no stores, people traded with one another to get the things they wanted or needed. If people wanted something that they could not get in their area, they traded with people in other areas. The Ohlone had many types of shells, beads that they made from shells, pine nuts, and salt. They traded these for arrowheads, strong wood to make weapons, and dyes to create paints. Since the trader acted as a representative of the whole tribe, he needed to be trusted by his tribespeople. The trader was such an important figure that when he arrived at different villages to trade, he was often welcomed with ceremonies and songs.

Ceremonies that included dancing and singing were performed for many occasions.

Another job that was very important to the Ohlone was basket weaving. Baskets were used for cooking, carrying water, and gathering and cooking acorns. Ohlone women used sticks and grass to make their baskets and often decorated them with shells and beads. The Ohlone considered basket weaving to be an art form.

Ohlone baskets were beautiful and strong.

Religion

The Ohlone believed in many different gods. This was because they believed that spirits lived in everything around them, including animals, trees, and the earth.

Every tribe had a shaman. A shaman was a powerful healer and spiritual leader. A shaman was believed to cure illness through medicine and prayer. If an Ohlone Indian fell sick, it was thought that an evil spirit caused the illness. The family of the sick person would hire a shaman to cure the illness, and he would try to do so by dancing, singing, and praying.

Music and dance were important parts of the Ohlone religion and culture. The Ohlone played instruments such as whistles, flutes, and rattles. They celebrated special occasions, including births, weddings, hunts, and religious days, with music and dancing. They also danced and sang to thank the gods for the things they had. The Ohlone believed that if they respected and celebrated what they took from nature, nature would be kind in return. When the Spanish arrived in California, the Ohlone way of life changed forever.

A shaman is a religious healer. ▶

The Founding of Mission Santa Cruz

The area around the San Lorenzo River was beautiful and lush. The banks of the river were covered with sycamore, cottonwood, and willow trees. Good pastures and forests were nearby as well. The land was very fertile, so there were many Ohlone Indian villages in the area. In 1790, the viceroy of New Spain asked Lasuén, who was then the president of the Alta California missions, to found a mission in this area. The viceroy gave him $1,000 to buy supplies and $400 to pay the travel expenses of the two friars who would live at the mission. Fray Lasuén did not want to establish the mission right away because he did not have all the necessary church ornaments. The viceroy promised that he would get them and asked Lasuén to borrow them from a nearby mission in the meantime.

On August 28, 1791, Fray Lasuén sprinkled holy water on the chosen site and named the 12th mission Santa Cruz, meaning Holy Cross. As with all the missions, a cross made of wood or twigs was set in the ground and a Mass was held. With Lasuén were six soldiers from the San Francisco presidio. Presidios were military forts for

A cross was placed in the ground during the founding ceremony.

The Spanish founded Mission Santa Cruz near many Ohlone villages.

soldiers built near mission sites. Also at the founding ceremony were a number of Ohlone Indians from nearby villages. Fray Lasuén wrote the viceroy to say that he was pleased at how many Indians had come and that he thought that many of them would gladly join the mission. Now Mission Santa Cruz was founded, but it was a few weeks before there was anything on the site but the wooden cross.

On September 24, 1791, California Indians from Mission Santa Clara de Asís came to Mission Santa Cruz to help put up temporary huts. The two friars who would live at the mission, Fray Isidro Alonzo Salazar and Fray Baldomero López, then had another founding ceremony. This time the ceremony was more formal and more people were there to see it. A chief from a nearby village, Chief Sugert,

Temporary shelters were built of wood.

After Indians were baptized, they were called neophytes.

brought his daughters and a few members of his tribe to the ceremony. They would be the first Indians converted to Christianity. The Spanish called the newly converted Indians neophytes. After the two friars held a Mass, the leader of the San Francisco presidio gave a speech, claiming the land for Spain. Then the soldiers fired their guns into the air and the founding ceremony was complete. The friars invited the Ohlone Indians to help build the temporary shelters, saying they would be paid with blankets and maize. The shelters went up quickly.

Mission Santa Cruz operated without any problems in its first few months. Animals, grains, and supplies were brought from other nearby missions so that the people at Mission Santa Cruz could begin farming. The friars celebrated their first baptism on October 9, 1791. A baptism is the ceremony that officially makes someone a Christian. Since the friars were at the mission to try to encourage as many people as possible to become Christians, they must have been very excited about this first conversion.

A few months later, the San Lorenzo River flooded. The buildings at Mission Santa Cruz were damaged. Instead of repairing the current mission site, the friars decided to rebuild nearby, on higher ground.

Farming was an important part of life at Mission Santa Cruz.

The mission had to be rebuilt and repaired because of flooding.

They were afraid that if they stayed where they were, the mission might be flooded again.

After the move, new temporary shelters had to be built. Although the mission had some problems, there were still a number of Ohlone Indians who wanted to join. By December 1791, the friars had baptized 19 adults and 68 children. The Ohlone had built

The Ohlone grew their own food at the mission.

temporary housing for the friars and a temporary church. Farming had also been successful, and they had fenced in the livestock and planted an orchard.

Once the basics of mission life were established, the Indians began building the permanent church. The soldiers taught the Ohlone how to make adobe bricks from a mixture of water, mud, and straw. This mixture was packed into rectangular molds and set in the sun to dry. Once the bricks were dry, they could be removed from the molds and stored until they were needed. On February 27, 1793, the cornerstone of the permanent church was laid. It would take over a year to finish the building. The Ohlone Indians worked hard building the foundation out of stone and building the walls out of the adobe bricks they had made. When the church was finished it was 30 feet wide, 112 feet long, and 25 feet high. The first Mass was held there on May 11, 1794.

Adobe bricks.

Life at Mission Santa Cruz

When the Ohlone Indians joined Mission Santa Cruz, their way of life changed a great deal. Indians who were baptized and converted to Christianity were called neophytes. Once baptized, the neophytes were not allowed to practice their own religion anymore. They also had to obey all the rules imposed on them by the friars. They were never allowed to leave the mission without permission. According to Spanish customs, women were locked in their quarters at night, and neophytes who did not do their work were beaten, put in leg irons, or jailed. The Indians had to give up their way of life, their religion, and their culture when they joined the mission. They gave up their freedom, too.

Unmarried women and girls over the age of nine lived together in the mission building, in an area called a *monjerío*. Much of the women's work was done in the *monjerío*. The women were not allowed to come outside of the building until they had finished all of their work. Families and unmarried men lived in housing just outside the mission, called *rancherías*.

◀ *Building the mission was hard work.*

The neophytes made roof tiles by molding them over logs.

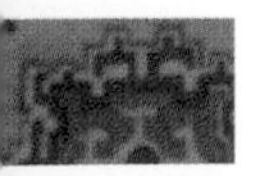

An average day at Mission Santa Cruz followed a strict schedule:

6:00 A.M.	The mission bells rang to wake everyone at the mission and at the *ranchería*.
6:00-6:30 A.M.	Time for prayers.
6:30 A.M.	Breakfast.
7:00 A.M.	The bells rang to call everyone to work.
12:00 P.M.	Lunch.
1:00 P.M.	A rest period, called a *siesta*.
3:00 P.M.	Everyone returned to work.
5:00 P.M.	Dinner.
6:00 P.M.	Evening prayers.
7:00 P.M.	Free time.
8:00 P.M.	Bedtime for women.
9:00 P.M.	Bedtime for men.

The Ohlone men worked at farming, building, blacksmithing, and making leather goods and tools. The women prepared food, spun thread, wove cloth, sewed, and made soap and candles. The friars taught religious studies to the children and went around to make sure that all the neophytes were doing their work and that none had run away from the mission.

Early Troubles at Mission Santa Cruz

Since Mission Santa Cruz was located near the San Lorenzo River, it began quite successfully. Crops were plentiful, thanks to the rich soil. Construction of the mission buildings continued. Large stones for a mill were ordered from the nearby Mission San Carlos Borromeo, and a millhouse was constructed. By the fall of 1796, the mill was built and running. Having a mill was important because now the mission could grind its own corn and flour for food. A granary was built to store grain, and rooms were built for weaving. That year, the missionaries recorded that 600 bushels of corn, 60 bushels of beans, and 1,200 bushels of grain were grown at the mission. Their crops were so plentiful that they even had extra to send to other missions, such as Mission San Carlos Borromeo. The livestock were healthy and had plenty to eat. The Indians worked hard at farming, weaving, blacksmithing, spinning, and making adobe bricks.

Although the mission was very productive, all was not well. Since the founding of the mission, a number of different friars had come to live and do missionary work there. Many were not happy and left after just a year or so. It seems that the Ohlone were not happy at the mission either. In 1796, one of the friars wrote to the presidio at San Francisco to ask for more soldiers to come and protect the mission from the threat of Indian attacks.

Mission Santa Cruz faced many problems in the years after its founding. ▶

The Hard Times Continue

Villa de Branciforte

The governor of Alta California decided to build a *pueblo*, or settlement, just across the river from Mission Santa Cruz in an effort to bring more Spanish settlers to the area. On May 12, 1797, nine settlers from New Spain arrived, and the town called Villa de Branciforte was established. Over the next year, more Spanish settlers came to the town. By September 1799, 40 men lived there. The governor had hoped to bring craftsmen who would start businesses and bring families to the town. Instead, the men at Villa de Branciforte did no work. They drank, played cards, and fought. The settlers used money to try to lure the Indians away from the mission so that they could use the Indians to help them work on their buildings or in their fields. The friars were upset that Villa de Branciforte had been built so close to their mission. They felt that the unruly settlers were a bad influence on the neophytes at Mission Santa Cruz.

The Neophytes Escape

In 1797, heavy rains destroyed part of the church and damaged some of the other buildings. Much work needed to be done in order to complete the repairs. Many neophytes were tired of working at the mission. They were unhappy there and missed the freedom of their old life in their villages. That year, 138 neophytes escaped from the mission. Some managed to hide from the soldiers who were sent to find them, but 90 Indians were hunted down and brought back to the mission. These neophytes were punished and forced to return to work.

◀ *The settlers at Villa de Branciforte drank and played cards instead of working.*

In 1798, 189 neophytes escaped, leaving only about 35 at the mission. The friars were distraught. The neophytes had run away. The mission's lands were overflowing with water. The livestock were dying. To top it all off, that year, a dead whale on the beach was attracting an unusually large number of wolves and bears, which were a threat to the farm animals in the area.

The friars asked for soldiers to come and help them rebuild their damaged mission. Work continued over the next few years. In 1810, a large *monjerío* with two wings was built for women and girls.

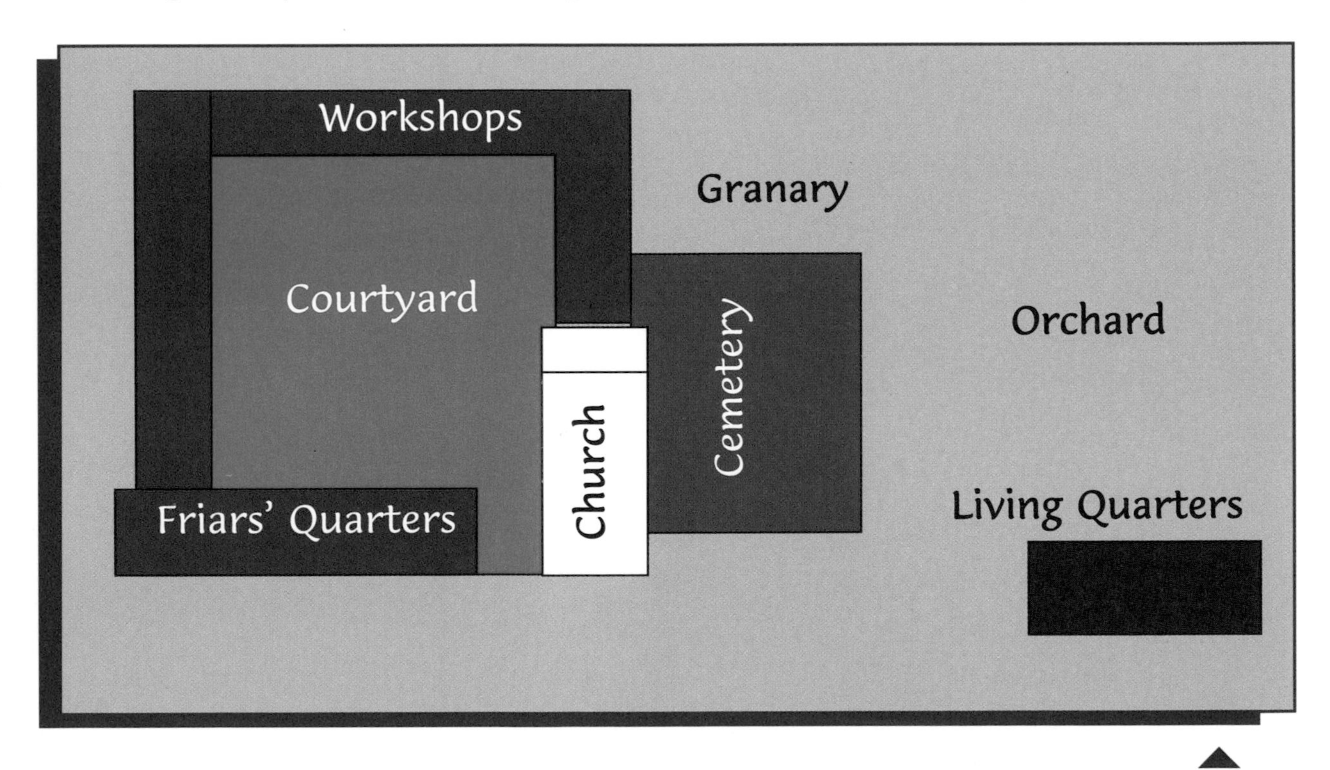

The layout of Mission Santa Cruz.

A Murder and the First Autopsy in California

On October 12, 1812, one of the friars at the mission, Fray Quintana, was found dead in his bed. He had been sick for some time, so it was believed that he died of natural causes.

Two years later, rumors that Fray Quintana had been murdered started to spread. The friar had not been a well-liked man. He was known to be cruel and had beaten neophytes with whips tipped with wire. His cruelty had led some neophytes to stop speaking Spanish and to stop working. The neophytes believed that he was inventing some kind of torture instrument to punish them even more.

A new investigation of the case began. An autopsy was performed on the body, and it was found that Fray Quintana had been hanged. It was decided that the friar had been called out of bed to help a sick man in the orchard. He was then surrounded by some neophytes who killed him. Nine neophytes were caught and blamed for the murder. Five were sentenced to 200 lashes with a whip and to work in chains for as long as 10 years. The others died in prison. The case and the punishment of the neophytes further damaged the relationship between the friars and the Ohlone Indians at Mission Santa Cruz.

Mission Santa Cruz Is Almost Lost

The Pirate Hippolyte de Bouchard

In 1818, the French pirate, Hippolyte de Bouchard, raided the presidio at Monterey. He and his crew stole many valuables and burned buildings there. It was feared that he was moving toward Mission Santa Cruz. On November 21, 1818, the governor of Alta California, Governor de Sola, ordered the friars at Mission Santa Cruz to move everyone out of the mission. Fray Ramon Olbés and all the neophytes went to Mission Santa Clara de Asís for safety.

Governor de Sola asked the Villa de Branciforte authorities if they would help pack up the valuables at the mission while the friars and the neophytes escaped to safety. The governor wanted to make sure that the valuables would not fall into the hands of the pirate Bouchard.

With the population of Mission Santa Cruz on its way to the nearby mission, the Villa de Branciforte settlers arrived. However, instead of safeguarding the valuables, the people of Villa de Branciforte stole the possessions for themselves. Then they looted and set fire to some of the mission buildings, even destroying sacred objects in the church. The pirate Bouchard never arrived at Mission Santa Cruz. Mission Santa Cruz was destroyed instead by the people of Villa de Branciforte.

◀ *Pirates attacked the presidio at Monterey, near Mission Santa Cruz.*

Diseases

Fray Olbés was very discouraged by the events unfolding at Mission Santa Cruz. He threatened to abandon the mission forever. After some of the Villa de Branciforte looters were caught and punished, he agreed to stay. Mission Santa Cruz, however, continued to have severe

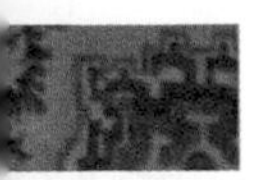

problems. European diseases were killing the neophytes. The California Indians had never been exposed to illnesses like measles, mumps, or scarlet fever, and their bodies could not fight them. The friars tried to find cures but were unsuccessful. Even the shamans couldn't help their people. Many neophytes who did not get sick were scared of the deadly diseases and ran away from the mission.

The Yokut Indians

Between those Indians who escaped and those who died from disease, the population of Mission Santa Cruz was shrinking. The missionaries spread out in the hills and tried to find new Indian tribes to move to the mission. They eventually came upon the Yokut tribe, but the Indians were not interested in joining the mission. Although it was against the law to force people to join the mission, it was done anyway. The Yokut were dragged against their will to Mission Santa Cruz.

The Yokut were as unhappy as the Ohlone had been, and like the Ohlone, they ran away. Hundreds of neophytes either escaped or died, causing Mission Santa Cruz to be one of the smallest missions in all of Alta California.

◀ *European diseases killed thousands of California Indians.*

Secularization

After many years of fighting with Spain, in 1821, New Spain finally became an independent country. It was renamed Mexico. The Mexican government wanted to return the mission lands to the California Indians and secularize the missions. This meant that the missions would not be run by missionaries anymore, but by parish priests. These priests would just be religious leaders and would not be able to make rules for the California Indians. All the work that the Spanish missionaries had done would be put to an end. The friars were strongly opposed to this secularization. They had originally intended to secularize the missions when they believed the Indians were ready to live on their own as loyal Spanish citizens. However, this day never came. The mission lands soon belonged to Mexican citizens who had to follow Mexican, not church, laws.

Mission Santa Cruz was one of the first missions to be secularized. The neophytes were told that they could leave the mission, and they were given some livestock to take with them. They were also supposed to own the land, but some Mexican officials cheated them, selling it to local ranchers instead.

The Ohlone had lived for too long at the mission to return to their old ways of life. Since the mission lands now belonged to Mexico, the Indians could no longer continue the farming and trades that they had learned there. The Ohlone population at the mission was hurt even more when an epidemic of smallpox swept through the area, killing many. The Indian population went from around 300 to a devastating 71. The remaining Indians tried to live off a small portion of land that was left, but they were eventually forced out by more new settlers.

◀ *This is what Mission Santa Cruz looked like in the 1820s.*

California Becomes a State

Alta California was becoming occupied by more and more American settlers. The United States fought a war with Mexico over the territory of Alta California, called the Mexican War. When the United States won in 1850, California became the 31st state. In 1859, President James Buchanan gave Mission Santa Cruz back to the Catholic church. However, much of the mission had been destroyed in an earthquake on January 9, 1857. In 1863, President Abraham Lincoln signed an act that stated that the 21 California missions were once again the property of the Catholic church, which they still are today.

President Buchanan. ▶

▲

After the Mexican War, California became part of the United States.

Mission Santa Cruz Today

A smaller version of Mission Santa Cruz's church can still be seen today. A copy of the mission church that was destroyed in the 1857 earthquake was built near the original site in 1931. There is a wing attached to the church that holds some artifacts from the original mission.

Since its founding, Mission Santa Cruz has been a part of the many changes that have taken place in California.

Today, the mission is a tourist attraction.

The small adobe building nearby was once housing for the neophytes. It is the only remaining mission housing left standing in California. It was built by the Yokut Indians in 1824. The housing was for Yokut families, especially families that had high-level workers, such as shoemakers, soapmakers, and other skilled craftsmen.

Blacksmithing and ranching exhibits are on display at the mission.

School groups come to the mission to make candles and tule mats.

This building became the headquarters of the Santa Cruz Mission State Historic Park. A museum was opened inside in 1991, 200 years after the mission was built, to teach people about mission life.

Today, you can visit this museum and participate in many activities. On certain days, you'll find volunteers dressed as people did 200 years ago. You can talk to the volunteers, help make candles, and learn part of California's rich and fascinating history.

Make Your Own Mission Santa Cruz

To make your own model of Mission Santa Cruz, you will need:

- cardboard
- glue
- masking tape
- toothpicks
- wire mesh
- beeswax sheets (from a craft store)
- white paint
- woodcraft sticks
- miniature gold bell
- corrugated cardboard
- X-Acto knife (Ask for an adult's help.)
- ruler

Directions

Step 1: Use a piece of cardboard at least 20″ by 15″ for your base.

Adult supervision is suggested.

Step 2: For the bell tower, cut out four pieces of cardboard to measure 8″ by 2″ each. Glue each piece to the base, so the edges form a cube. Hold each piece in place until the glue dries.

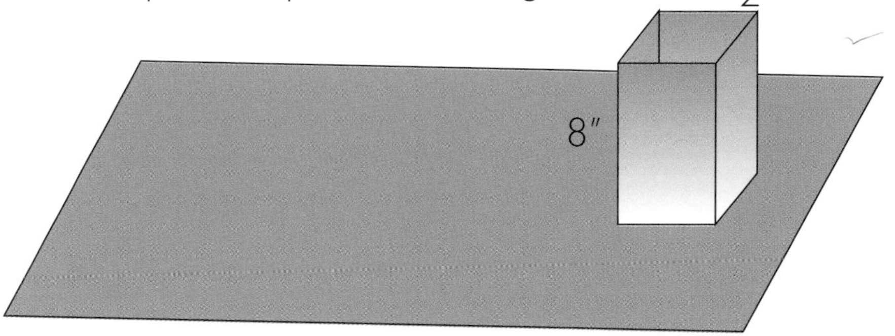

Step 3: Cut a piece of cardboard to measure 2″ by 2″, and glue it on top of the tower. Then cut four pieces of cardboard to measure 2″ by 1.5″ each. Cut an arch shape in each piece.

Step 4: Glue these pieces, one at a time, to the top of your tower in the shape of a square. Let dry. Place bell on a toothpick, and glue toothpick between two arches.

Step 5: Cut two pieces of cardboard to measure 6.6" by 8.6" each. These will be the front and back of the church.

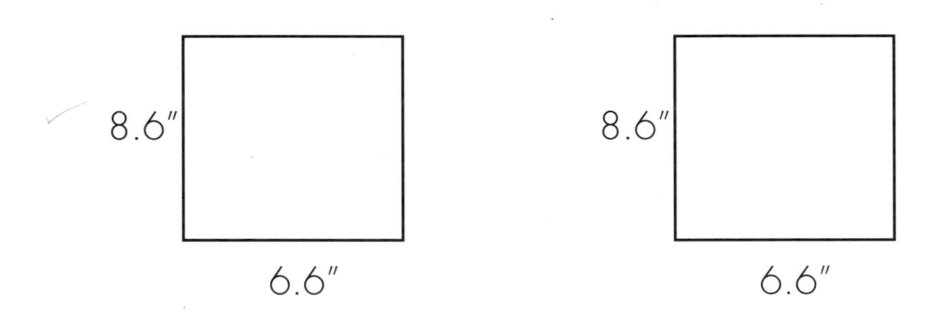

Step 6: Measure 3" down from the top and mark with a pencil on both sides. Cut diagonally from this mark to the midpoint at the top, forming a triangular shape.

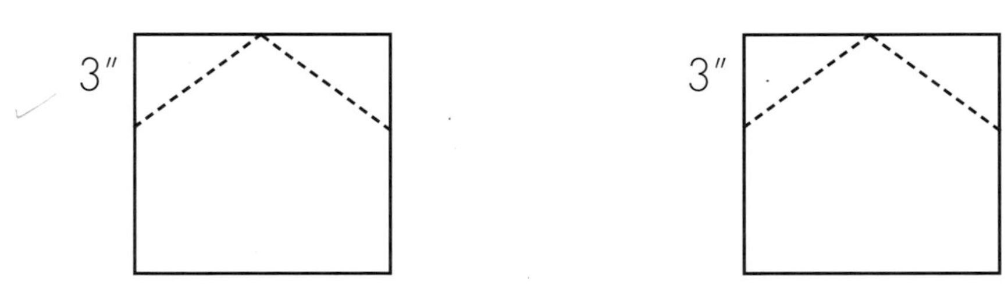

Step 7: Cut two pieces of cardboard to measure 5.6" by 13" each for the sides of the church. Glue all four sides in a square shape next to the tower. Hold each piece until the glue dries.

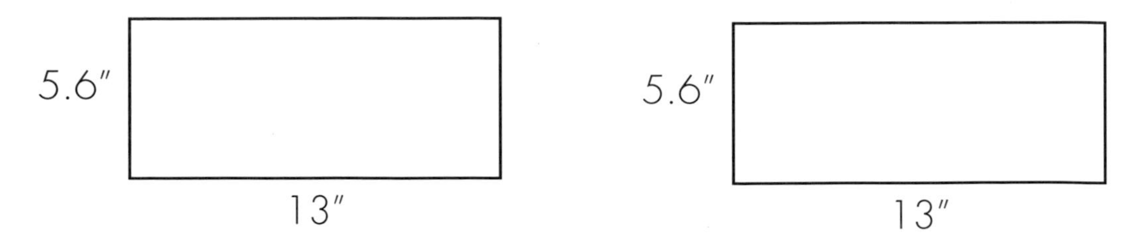

Step 8: To make the friars' quarters, cut three pieces of cardboard to measure 3.6" by 10" each for the front, back, and top.

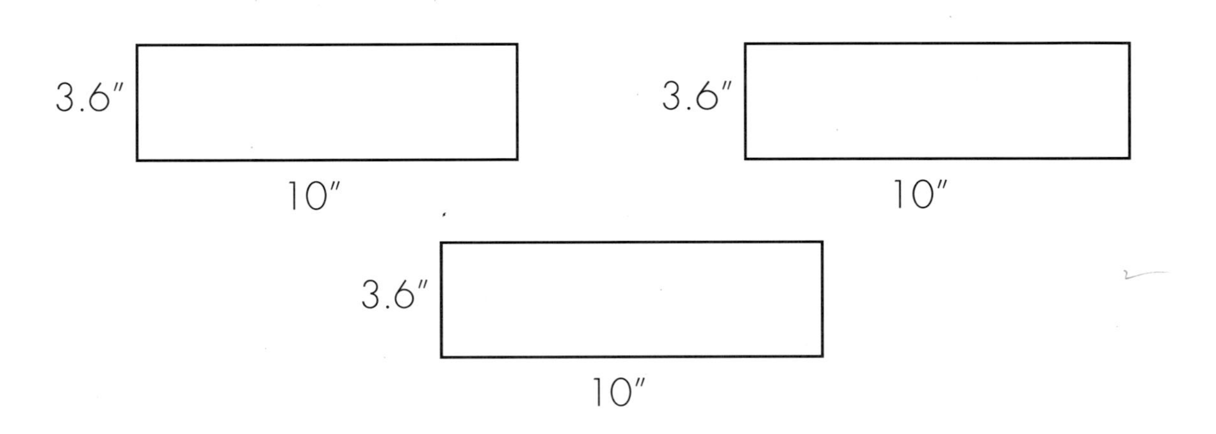

Step 9: In one of these pieces, cut out a door and three or four windows with an X-Acto knife. Glue two toothpicks inside the windows in a "t" shape.

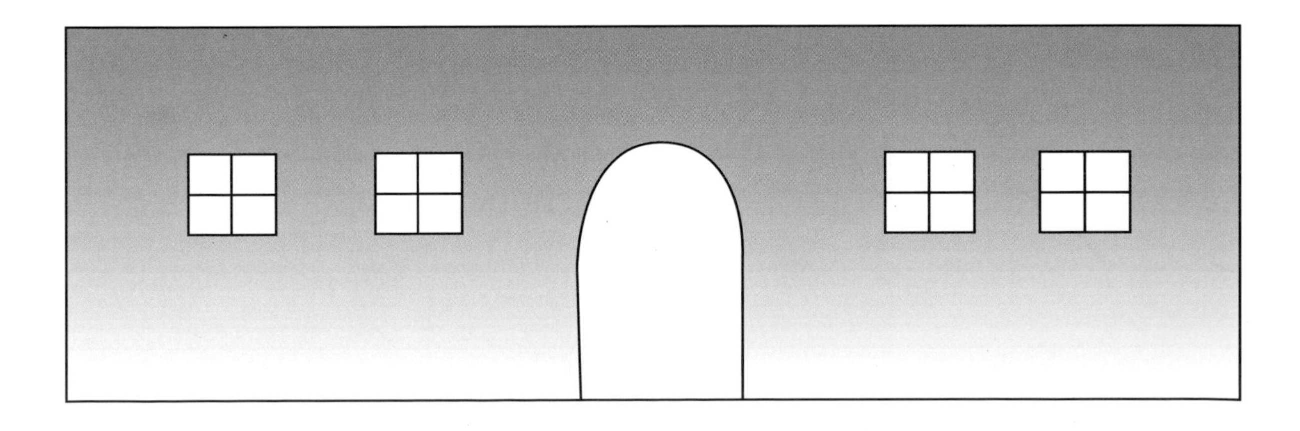

Step 10: Cut another piece of cardboard to measure 3.6" by 3.6". This is the left wall of the building (the church will make up the right side). Tape the sides together.

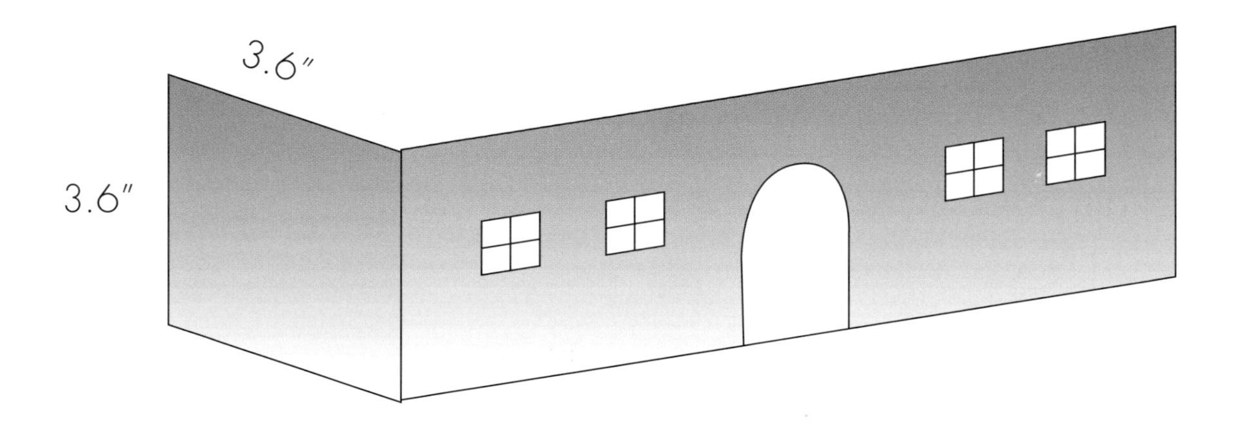

Step 11: Cut a piece of beeswax to measure 8.6" by 14". Bend in half, the long way, and glue to the top of the church. This is the roof.

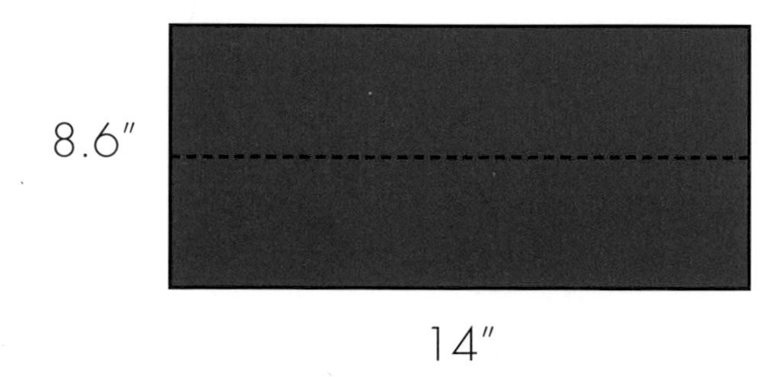

Step 12: Cut wire mesh in a circle that is 4" in diameter. Shape into half a ball and cover with small piece of beeswax. Place on top of the tower. Make a cross out of two toothpicks and stick it in the beeswax.

Step 13: Cut three woodcraft sticks in half lengthwise. Glue three together end to end. Repeat for the other three. These will be the top and bottom of the porch.

Step 14: Cut two woodcraft sticks in half and then lengthwise. Glue these between the two longer strips of sticks. Tape them in front of the friars' quarters.

Step 15: Cut a piece of corrugated cardboard for the church door. Cut a piece of beeswax 6" by 14.6" for the roof of the friars' quarters and glue in place. Decorate as you wish with miniature flowers and trees.

*Use the above mission as a reference for building your mission.

Important Dates in Mission History

1492	Christopher Columbus reaches the West Indies
1542	Cabrillo's expedition to California
1602	Sebastián Vizcaíno sails to California
1713	Fray Junípero Serra is born
1769	Founding of San Diego de Alcalá
1770	Founding of San Carlos Borromeo del Río Carmelo
1771	Founding of San Antonio de Padua and San Gabriel Arcángel
1772	Founding of San Luis Obispo de Tolosa
1775–76	Founding of San Juan Capistrano
1776	Founding of San Francisco de Asís
1776	Declaration of Independence is signed
1777	Founding of Santa Clara de Asís
1782	Founding of San Buenaventura
1784	Fray Serra dies
1786	Founding of Santa Bárbara Virgen y Mártir
1787	Founding of La Purísima Concepción de Maria Santísima
1791	**Founding of Santa Cruz** and Nuestra Señora de la Soledad
1797	Founding of San José, San Juan Bautista, San Miguel Arcángel, and San Fernando Rey de España
1798	Founding of San Luis Rey de Francia
1804	Founding of Santa Inés Virgen y Mártir
1817	Founding of San Rafael Arcángel
1823	Founding of San Francisco de Solano
1849	Gold found in northern California
1850	California becomes the 31st state

Glossary

adobe (uh-DOH-bee) Sun-dried bricks made of straw, mud, and sometimes manure.

Alta California (AL-tuh kal-ih-FOR-nee-uh) The area where the Spanish settled missions, today known as the state of California.

baptism (BAP-tih-zum) A ceremony performed when someone accepts the Christian faith, intended to cleanse the person of his sins.

Christian (KRIS-chun) Someone who follows the teachings of Jesus Christ and the Bible.

colonizing (KAH-luh-nyz-ing) When people from one part of the world settle another region.

convert (kun-VERT) To change religious beliefs.

Franciscan (fran-SIS-kin) A member of a Catholic religious group started by Saint Francis of Assisi in 1209.

friar (FRY-ur) A brother in a communal religious order. Friars can also be priests.

Mass (MAS) The main religious ceremony of the Catholic church.

missionary (MIH-shu-nayr-ee) A person who teaches his or her religion to people with different beliefs.

neophyte (NEE-oh-fyt) A person who has converted to another religion.

New Spain (NOO SPAYN) The area where the Spanish colonists had their capital in North America and that would later become Mexico.

presidio (prih-SEE-dee-oh) A military fort built near a mission site.

secularization (seh-kyuh-luh-rih-ZAY-shun) A process by which the mission lands were made to be non-religious.

shaman (SHAH-min) Medicine man, believed to use magic to heal the sick and to control other events in peoples lives.

viceroy (VYS-roy) The governor of a place who is there ruling as a representative of the king.

Pronunciation Guide

fray (FRAY)

monjerío (mohn-HAYR-ee-oh)

Ohlone (oh-LOH-nee)

pueblo (PWAY-bloh)

rancherías (RAHN-cher-EE-as)

siesta (see-EHS-tah)

temescal (TEH-mes-cal)

Resources

To learn more about the California missions, check out these books, videos, and Web sites:

Books

Genet, Donna. *Father Junípero Serra: Founder of the California Missions*. Springfield, NJ: Enslow Publishers, 1996.

Keyworth, C.L. *The First Americans: California Indians*. New York, NY: Facts on File, 1991.

Young, Stanley. *The Missions of California*. San Francisco, CA: Chronicle Books, 1998.

Videos

Missions of California: Father Junípero Serra.
Produced by Chip Taylor Productions
This 11-minute, full-color video features pictures of Father Serra, detailed maps, and scenery from many of the missions he founded. Should be available in your library. You can order by calling 1-800-876-CHIP.

Web Sites

www.escusd.k12.ca.us/missiontrail.html
www.jspub.comb/~jsp/teachers.html
www.csd.k12.ca.us/coyote_canyon/4/missions/mission_ndex.html

Index